My Salvation

Lorwin Marie S. Baculanta

Ukiyoto Publishing

Dedication

I dedicate this book to my family and friends. Especially to Dr. Ma. Lorna, my mother, who gave me support, to Jade, my sister, who gave me courage and to Dr. Edwin, my late father who gave me inspiration.

Contents

My Savior

-*Soldier*

Feeling cold as Ice
I see no meaning in life
All I do is hide

I wished to the stars
For them to shine, very bright
Guiding to the side

Oh Dear God, help me
For this soul has never loved
Someone strong and wise

Millions of bullets
Raging fires burning the grass
The bombs have been set

Boom! Where are you now?
A place where it's dark and far

My Salvation

"***Who are you?***" I said

"***Oh! me? Just a friend***"

He took my hand then we ran

What is this feeling?

I see now the view

"***Come.***" He said, climbing to Peak

I see now, He is...

Filipino-American Alliance

-*Soldier*

I'm sorry, I lied

Night, Can I be forgiven?

For I have trespassed

The wide galaxy

Shan't cease to make me believe

that hope is so near

Stars, where are you now?

I need light for the others

Reach! my brave comrade

Yes! I shall return

For you People are in need

I left them with hope

Battle has begun

Our Savior, where are you now?

Hopelessly, marching

My Salvation

The Rising Sun killed

Millions of people cried

Finish this wretched war

Nineteen Forty-Five

Finally, it has ended

Cheers! Let's celebrate

Fallen Soldier
-Soldier

I am a soldier

Fighting for my country men

Loyal, kind and loved...

I fight for what's right
I fight to protect their smiles

I fight for no tears

I'll do everything

For a good and bright future
Please remember me

Fallen Flame
Stained with blood

All is sad

Hope is gone

For we are done

A fleeting dream

Where heaven is real

Unfortunate, it seems

These wounds won't heal

How notorious they are

Willing to go that far

Without a care for the victims

Thus, all are out of rhythm

Killed for satisfaction

Without hesitation

A fruitless action

'Cause of collision

Whatever it may be
It's disarray we see
They fight and clash
Fire turned to ash

The ashes that we owned
By the wind, it was blown
The flame that was once here
Burned to our minds, so clear

Reunion
-*Soldier's Wife*

Many years have passed
As a survivor of war
Who am I to judge?

The scars that were marked
In both my mind and heart
Have always been apart

To forgive is hard
The cause of my loss of him
Tears made my eyes blur

I visited his grave
Lit up the candle to pray
"*Rest in peace, my love*"

I feel the wind blow

"*Thank you.*" Shocked, I turned around
I see his warm smile

Refuse to believe
Gently, he caressed my cheek
"*I miss you, my love*"

"*I don't have much time.*"
I gave him a kiss and say
"*I love you. Goodbye*"

My Hero
-Soldier's Child

"Where is my father?"
I often ask dear mother
"He is in our hearts."

"Never forgotten."
She said as she touched her chest
Showed a painful smile

"Child, you know nothing."
Said a voice I do not know
Oddly familiar

"Who is it?" I ask
"Know nothing for you'll be safe."
I don't understand

Time passed by quickly
I grew up with no father
Sometimes felt alone

Mother always works
For me, she always does all
For us to live on

Father may be gone
Leaving us a will to live
He is my hero

Light Of Hope
-*Soldier*

Fighting and clashing

Do you think this will bear fruit?

Nothing will happen

Yes, only despair

Will await in the future

Please, I beg of you

Let go and forgive

I hope you'll find resolve

Accept those feelings

You must pay no mind

To those nightmares you have dreamt

Overcome your fear

The sacrifices

Who fought and never gave up

Will not be in vain

I know, it's been years
Slowly, it will disappear
The grudge that you hold

You can start anew
By then, we can achieve peace
Go forward, my friend

A Promise For You
-*Soldier's Sibling*

Every action made

Follows some consequences

"Don't worry. " He said

Who am I to blame?

All of us suffered the same

We lose someone dear

My brother is gone

Leaving a wife and a child

"What to do?" I said

Really, I am lost

What am I supposed to do?

A thought came in mind

I'll do the right thing

In his stead, I will be there

For his dear loved ones

I'll be their pillar
Giving them support and love
If it's all for you

I've made up my mind
Those two will never be harmed
I promise you that

Sanity
-*Soldier*

If I were to choose

Which is right and which is wrong?

I'm afraid to lose

A lovely blossom
Hardly unnoticeable
Emanating worth

Symbol of virtue

Its sweet scent purifies me

Proving its true worth

A choice must be made

Doing the wrong, I can keep

If it's right, I'll lose

Something I long for

That comes with three syllables

It's second to none

Irreplaceable
The only thing that holds me
Unless, once it's gone

In this corrupt world
Even though it's for myself
Whether right or wrong

Whatever happens
I'll project my sincerity
In my every action

My Final Goodbye
-*Soldier*

There are many things
I've always wanted to do
Feelings to be felt

I've always held back
For my country and loved ones
I'll do everything

To keep them secured
There may be consequences
I'll keep on fighting

Until we find peace
Until there are no more tears
I'll stop as soon as

I can see their smiles
Until the weights are lifted
I can hear them laugh

Until that day comes
I don't have any regrets

Unfortunately

There is one regret
The only regret I have
And that is to leave

I am so sorry
I left instead of living
I may be selfish

But please don't forget
My tears, my laughter, my love
Will always be true

About the Author

Lorwin Marie S. Baculanta

Lorwin is the youngest daughter of a single-parent family. She lives together with her mother and sister in Tarlac. Her father died before she was born but the gap her father left is filled by her mother and sister's love. Lorwin used to play instruments such as piano and violin. She dislikes strawberries.

9 789360 169961